shot glass confessional

shot glass confessional

parker lee

Also by Parker Lee

(as Cyrus Parker)

poetry

DROPKICKromance
masquerade
coffee days whiskey nights

anthologized works

"Where the Sea Meets the Sky"
featured in
[Dis]Connected: Poems & Stories of Connection and Otherwise

A note from Parker

On December 10th, 2020 I announced on social media that I had started the process of having my name legally changed to better match my identity, something I had been contemplating for several years but was too afraid to pursue. To coincide with my legal name change, I also decided to change the name I publish under, dropping the pseudonym I've used professionally for over a decade, Cyrus Parker.

Publishing is interesting in that it simultaneously moves very fast and very slow. While a decision like this absolutely impacts me in the present tense, it's something that may not be seen in my traditionally published work for *at least* another year. As someone who is very impatient, I decided to circumvent that wait by altering my existing self-published work, *shot glass confessional*, to reflect my new name, Parker Lee.

If you picked up the first edition of this book, you may or may not notice some changes in the order of the poems and some changes to the poems themselves. If you're new here, welcome to the revised edition, which—in my opinion—flows much better than it did originally. In either case, thank you for taking a chance on my work. I appreciate it—and you—more than you know.

With love,
Parker

*for those of us who have ever
been made to doubt our own worth.*

Content Warning

shot glass confessional contains sensitive material relating to the following topics:

alcohol use, toxic relationships, and potentially more.

Please remember to practice self-care before, during, and after reading.

genesis

/ˈjenəsəs/
noun

beginning. origin.

i've long since stopped
believing in things
i cannot see,
so now i pray to my pen
because only my words
can set me free.

you and me?
we were supposed to be
the type of romance
that even the poets
struggle to put into words.

unfortunately, there is only tragedy to be found here.

do you remember that night?
when we booked a hotel room
in hell's kitchen, got wine drunk
at a fancy restaurant, and ordered
way too many desserts? that night,
the 27th floor felt like the top of the world,
but now all i can think about is how
magnificent our inevitable fall was.

i suppose i should've known something was
wrong when the valentine's day card i sent you
showed back up in my mailbox a week later. on
valentine's day, no less. but in typical fashion, i
blamed myself. maybe i got the address wrong.
maybe i was moving too fast. maybe you didn't
feel the same way about me that i felt about you. i
never did find out what really happened because
we never talked about it. and we didn't talk about
it because i didn't really want to know. i just
wanted to go on thinking we were okay.

i thought this relationship was going to be symbiotic, but i'm beginning to think one of us is a parasite, and spoiler alert: it isn't me.

you've declared yourself a martyr
of love, but you're no saint.
we both have blood on our hands—
the difference is, only one of us
is willing to admit it.

call me idealistic.
call me a daydreamer.
call me starry-eyed.
call me a fool.
call me what you'd like,
believe what you want to believe,
because it can never change
who i know myself to be.

my regrets are many, and i've
said "i'm sorry" more times
than i've said "i love you."

which is to say i'm sorry
i didn't love you more
than you loved being right.

kindness is not transactional.
never let anyone make you
feel like you're indebted to them
because they showed you the most
basic form of human decency.

we're not so different, you and i,
and it makes me wonder if you
resent yourself for all your mistakes
as much as you've made me
resent myself for all of mine.

the little bit of self-confidence
i had left is gone and i have you
to thank for that.

i thought i had
finally found my place in this
fucked up world,

but now the only thing i know
how to do is second guess
every single decision i make.

if you want to see me
thrive,
back me into a corner.
doubt me.
give me no
other option
but to prove you
wrong.

i get that i can be too much sometimes,
but i refuse to ever make myself small for anyone.
not even you.

if i took a shot every time
the blame has been passed around,
i would've passed out a long time ago.

it was my birthday, and there wasn't a single acknowledgement of it from you. no card, no call, not even a text. but i didn't let that ruin my day. i took myself out for breakfast, got a booth all to myself, and ordered a big stack of pumpkin pancakes with a carafe of coffee on the side. after i paid the bill, i went shopping and bought myself some new boots and the leather jacket i had been eyeing for the last month. i read a book, and i wrote some poems. i poured myself a drink, and i gave a toast. to me, the only person whose love i ever truly needed.

i have discovered that it is possible to both
find yourself and lose yourself
at the exact same time.

water the seeds.
tear out the weeds.
feed the new growth.
starve what threatens it.

i can't seem to pinpoint the last time i saw you, and i don't know if that's a good thing or a bad thing. memories fade, and moments, no matter how significant they might seem at the time, become nothingness. just like we did.

i don't know if you can even call this a breakup
when there was no true breaking point. we just
drifted apart, like a boat from the shore, so far
from each other that not even the beckoning of a
lighthouse could guide us back together.

i'm treading water, barely able to keep my head above the surface, but you don't seem concerned. you've always been too preoccupied swimming with the sharks to pay me any attention anyway.

i gave you the very best pieces of me, and it still wasn't enough for you. now i'm stitching those pieces back together to make something even greater—me, whole, without you.

you only have one heart.
protect it like your life depends on it.

i am not bitter.
i hold no resentment
in this heart.
if anything,
i am grateful.
grateful for
the lesson learned
in trusting
the wrong people.

you owe them nothing
least of all your silence,

so never feel guilty for
speaking your mind.

some days, i am kinder to myself than i am on others. progress is progress, no matter how incremental it might be. remember to stop and celebrate these small victories, too, because they are just as important as the big ones.

i've learned that my failures
do not define me. i sing them
like the refrain of a hymn
and sometimes, that is enough.

i've also learned on the days it isn't,
you must change your perspective
because you tried,
and that is a success of its own.

if they don't believe in you,
then find someone else who does,
even if that someone is yourself.

whenever you feel lost, say these words:

i am more than this.
i am more than this.
i am *so much* more than this.

and repeat them as many times as you need.

someone can be overflowing with self-love
and not know how to love another,
so who is to say that the opposite cannot
be true? never let anyone convince you
that you are not worthy of another's love
because you haven't learned self-love yet.
you have always been worthy.

i discovered my own worth
a very long time ago, but
at some point on the journey
to get here, i misplaced it and
forgot it existed. out of sight,
out of mind, as they often say.
now, i'm retracing my steps,
rediscovering just what it was
i lost, and i am striving to become
the best version of myself that
has ever worn this skin.

the death of us was my biggest fear. you had me convinced that no one could ever love me the way you could, and you clipped my wings before letting me go to ensure i would never get too far. since then, i've not only figured out how to fly again, but i'm soaring higher than ever before.

crows are said to be some of the most intelligent
creatures in the entire world. they remember the
faces of those who have shown them a kindness,
and they never forget the face of one who has
wronged them. i think there's a lesson to be
learned here when it comes to deciding who
should and shouldn't be given your forgiveness.
be soft, but not too soft.

i am not perfect, but i am a perfect mess.
sometimes i say the wrong things.

sometimes i drink a little too much.
sometimes i hurt the people i care about most.

your mistakes do not define who you are,
but if you do not own them, they will own you.

break the cycle and be a better you
than you were yesterday.

my cat knows none of the good or bad i've done in my life, yet she is always by my side. i don't think i could ever be the person she thinks i am, but i'll be damned if i don't try to be.

ask for forgiveness,
then forgive yourself.

you texted me at midnight
on new year's eve
and i left you on read,
but you'll never know it
because i turned off
receipts a long time ago.
this year, i'm taking
back my power,
and that means you
don't get to know
anything about me
anymore.

i've spent far too much of my life
listening to that little voice in the back of my head
that tells me i'm not good enough.
i am good enough. i'm more than good enough,
and i'm not sure you'll ever see that,
but i do, and that's what's really important.

i used to write poetry with a pencil.
it's not that i have commitment issues,
i just needed to know erasing
my mistakes was an option.

but you can't learn from your mistakes
by pretending they never happened,
so i picked up a pen and, with bold strokes,
began owning all of mine.

my story does not end with you.
no, you were merely the prologue.
this is a new beginning, the first chapter
of the first book in the series
that will inevitably be known as my life.

those thoughts hanging heavy on your heart?
write them down. speak them out loud. breathe
life into them and give them wings. timing is
everything. moments pass in the blink of an eye,
and with it, the chance for your words to mean
something to someone, somewhere.

to be a poet is to be honest.
to be a poet is to tell your truths,
because if you don't, then who will?

i used to think blowing up bridges was enough to protect me from the ones i've had to distance myself from, but that was never the solution. people will find their way to you one way or another, so instead, i am building bigger bridges to better places—places that can only be reached by taking the high road.

some people would sooner watch you burn
than reach out a hand to pull you from
the fire. it is in those moments you must
swallow the flames and become a phoenix—
mighty enough to reduce the world to ash.
merciful enough not to.

fight for what you want.
wage war for what you need.

keep
climbing that
mountain, even if it means
falling, picking yourself back up,
and starting again from the very bottom.

when they ask me how the view is,
i tell them that the city twinkles like
starlight at night, and that is not a lie.
it *is* a nice view, but it's just a view.
ask me instead what lies beneath it.
ask me about the secrets whispered
in the deepest darkest alleyways.
ask me how the locals behave when
they think nobody is watching them.
no, don't ask me about the view—
ask me what it takes to survive there.

the days are starting to get longer again.
there was a time i thought the chill would
never leave these bones, but there is warmth
inside of me that you will never feel
because i've finally realized that i never
needed anyone to light up the world for me—
i can be my own sunlight, and no one
can ever tell me i am burning too brightly.

moving on is not always easy,
but darling, it is always worth it.

love is a wonderful thing,
but it isn't the only wonderful thing.

there is the scent of fresh coffee,
and the sound of a cat's purr.

there are autumn sunrises,
and summer sunsets.

there is that moment after a snowfall
where the air is still

and the whole world is perfectly
covered in a soft white blanket.

there are clear blue afternoons
and star-filled midnights.

there is realizing for the first time
that your value has never been

and will never be dependent
on how another feels about you.

you are worthy today.
you will be worthy tomorrow.

a lot can happen between the first sip of coffee and the last drop of whiskey. beginnings and endings are both important, but never forget to savor the moments in between. drink in every last drop life has to offer, because you deserve to live it to the fullest.

fin.

Acknowledgments

amanda, for being my everything.

You, for supporting my passion.

Those who doubted me, for making me fight harder.

And a special thank you to Aaron Kent, who inspired the very first poem in the book. the original can be found in *Poetic Interviews*, available from Broken Sleep Books.

About the Author

Parker Lee (formerly known as Cyrus Parker) is a non-binary poet and storyteller, as well as the author of multiple collections of poetry, including their latest, *coffee days whiskey nights*. Hailing from a small coastal town in New Jersey alongside wife and poetess amanda lovelace—as well as their three cats—Parker can almost always be found at home, not writing when they should be, drinking too much coffee, and pretending their kitchen is their favorite café.

website: www.byparkerlee.com
twitter: @itsparkerlee
instagram: @itsparkerlee

Now Available

from Central Avenue Publishing
www.centralavenuepublishing.com

Made in the USA
Middletown, DE
23 August 2022